Rain

A POEM

Gurgle down the spout.
Gush through the drain.
Swirl along the gutter.
Down comes the rain.

On go our raincoats —
outside in a flash.
Find the biggest puddle.
SPLASH! SPLASH!
SPLASH!

Worms on the driveway.
Snails on the grass.
Watch them slide and glide
in a drip-drop dance.

7

Rain on the houses.
Rain on the trees.
Rain on the animals.
Rain on you and me!